Making Love Work *while* Leading Your Family
WORKBOOK

A Companion Guide for Couples & Individuals Preparing for Marriage

DRS. SAMUEL, JR., & ANDREA
HAYES

Authors of the #1 International Best Seller

Making Love Work While Leading Your Family:
A Companion Guide for Couples

Websites: www.ThePensieroPress.com | www.LentzLeadership.com
Twitter: https://twitter.com/drcheryllentz
Facebook: https://www.facebook.com/Dr.Cheryl.Lentz

All rights reserved. No part of this book may be reproduced or transmitted in any form or by any means, graphic, electronic or mechanical, including photocopying, recording, taping, Web distribution, or by any informational storage and retrieval system without written permission from the publisher except for the inclusion of brief quotations in a review or scholarly reference.

Books are available through Pensiero Press at special discounts for bulk purchases for the purpose of sales promotion, seminar attendance, or educational purposes.

Copyright © 2020 by Pensiero Press

Volume ISBN: 978-1-7356817-1-9

*Kindle and electronic versions available

Cover design & interior: Gary Rosenberg • www.thebookcouple.com

CONTENTS

Preface v

Introduction 1

How to Use This Workbook 3

SESSION 1. LOVE & LEAD: YOU 5

SESSION 2. LOVE & LEAD: VALUE 27

SESSION 3. LOVE & LEAD: COMMUNICATION 41

SESSION 4. LOVE & LEAD: CONFLICT 55

SESSION 5. LOVE & LEAD: INTIMACY 67

Group Leader Insights 77

About the Authors 79

Key Word Index 81

This workbook is dedicated to couples who have and are overcoming problems in their marriages and to single readers who desire a Godly marriage. Your continued dedication to making your marriage an example for others is truly admired and appreciated. This tool was created for those who will pave the way for the next generation of married couples through their example by following God's plan for marriage.

PREFACE

*A*fter 20 plus years of marriage and many ups and downs, we want to not only acknowledge our journey, but also help others along the way. Throughout the many challenges, God made a way for us to enjoy each other and grow closer together.

In our book, *Making Love Work While Leading Your Family*, we unpack our experiences, marriage lessons, and leaderships insight for you. We highlight the good, the bad, and the ugly illustrating how the Word of God helped us through our dark moments. From those difficult times, we grew into overcomers to strengthen our marriage.

Now, we turn from us to you. Building upon our book, we focused this workbook on you and your goals for your marriage. It is designed with you in mind to grow as a person and a couple through reflection and exercises that will assist you with getting closer to God and your spouse.

Based on feedback from close friends and others who have read our book, we have gained insight from several individuals who are single. Many of single individuals expressed that the book helped them reflect on past relationships and focus on what they may do differently to improve their next relationship to hopefully lead to marriage. Taking into consideration the helpful feedback we have received, we decided to make the workbook interactive not only for married couples, but for single readers as well.

Helping others along the way means for us to create a place to grow stronger in marriage God's way. In our marriage ministry, we do our part to help forge strong marriages. We believe and teach biblical principles for marriage and hope they bless your lives as they did ours.

INTRODUCTION

*M*arriage is a special institution that is not only sacred but is something that should be entered into mutually. One of the things that we highlighted in our book is the importance of being united as one and making sure there is open communication and the willingness to respect other's feelings. Communication is essential because throughout this workbook, not only will we focus on effective communication with your significant other but also on the importance of honestly communicating with yourself.

This workbook is designed to help enhance relationships. As couples work through this workbook, it is our goal to help with the enrichment of your relationship and the development of more specific goals for your future. For individuals who are single, the hope is that you will consider the things that you look for in a significant other as you continue to improve yourself.

We hope that this workbook will not only be used to accompany our book but can serve as a guide for the continued growth in your relationship or future relationship(s). The activities and interactive questions are designed to help add thought provoking insights based on your personal experiences. We pray that it can be a resource for many years to come. As you complete it, it will be personalized towards you and your relationship or future relationship(s).

HOW TO USE THIS WORKBOOK

This workbook is designed to address many different situations. It helps with the single person who wants to get married by helping them work through potential challenges they may face once they are married. It aids the married couples by helping them reflect and positioning them to be able to overcome their current challenges while working towards their future. It can also assist a group leader with their relationship goals for the group. Addressing these situations can be done through our session format.

Session Format

There are 5 sessions in this workbook with two parts each. Part One deals with reflection focused on preparing your mind for the task at hand. Part Two allows you to complete actions steps, focused on you, your relationship, and your future.

Couples Insights

As you and your significant other work through the workbook, it is very important that you are honest and respond genuinely. This workbook was created to enhance your relationship and appreciate your partner for the role that he or she plays in your life. We invite you to use this workbook as a guide to help not only improve your relationship as a whole but to help you as individuals understand your part in the relationship.

Singles Insights

Not only was this workbook intended for couples, but we considered singles as well. It is very important that singles use this workbook as a reflection point considering past relationships to look at the positive and the negative aspects to help provide a guide for future relationships. We encourage you to consider the things that you look for in a partner and to also reflect on the things within yourself that someone may admire or even dislike. While working through the book, you will notice that we address couples and partners, please consider how you would respond as you prepare yourself for your spouse. We also invite you to consider past relationships and how you or your partner responded in various situations. We hope that you are able to use this workbook as a guide while keeping in mind that as you complete the tasks presented, they are based upon your personal experiences.

SESSION 1.
LOVE & LEAD: YOU

Based on Chapter 1 of *Making Love Work While Leading Your Family*, "Your Spouse is not You: Unrealistic Expectations."

Session's Challenge: Knowing who you are as an individual can help add to the unity that you have as a pair; thus, allowing you, as a couple, to leverage God's blueprint to create a path to success.

Self-reflection

Married Couples: What is a characteristic that you most admire about your spouse?

Singles: What is a characteristic that you look for in a partner?

Opening Prayer

God our Father,
I know that I am fearfully and wonderful made (Ps. 139:14) in your image (Gen. 1:27). Help me to remember that You know me, and I can be real with you about my challenges.

As I go on this journey to better myself and build a stronger marriage, help me to understand that You guide my footsteps (Ps. 119:133). Help me to grow closer to You and process my thoughts and feelings that I encounter along the way.

Lord, allow me to love my spouse through the honest conversations (1 Peter 4:8). Please be with our hearts Lord, as we face our present reality working towards our future. Allow our marriage to honor and glorify You.
In Jesus' name, Amen!

NOTES

Nugget: Completing this session requires transparency with yourself and God.

Scriptures: Psalms 139:1-3
O Lord, you have searched me and know me. You know when I sit down and when I rise up; you discern my thoughts from far away. You search out my path and my lying down and are acquainted with all my ways.

Yolanda Adams
"Open Up My Heart"

PART ONE: REFLECTION

In Chapter 1, we encountered problems from our upbringing, dating, and the early years of marriage. To help us deal with the problems presented in Figure 1, the Word of God urged us to shift our mindsets to Him. We saw the opportunities versus the problems that we faced.

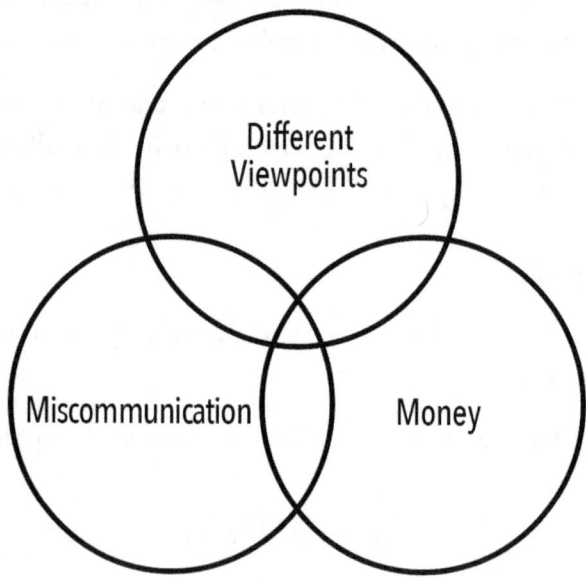

Scriptures: 1 Peter 5:7 Cast all your anxiety on him, because he cares for you.

Figure 1. Chapter 1's central themes with our problems, lessons, and insights.

Coming to terms with our role in our relationship and our different viewpoints was essential to the growth in our marriage. Along with the expectations that we put on each other, we had to realize that although we were legally married, we had to work to solidify our union and come together as one. We had to do this while working towards our thoughts on money and communication.

As you focus on your marriage or future relationship, consider the significant challenges that you have faced and the way they may have caused an impact. List three challenges that each of you have faced in your marriage or anticipate facing when you become married.

SESSION 1. LOVE & LEAD: YOU

HUSBAND

1. _____
_____
_____

2. _____
_____
_____

3. _____
_____
_____

WIFE

1. _____
_____
_____

2. _____
_____
_____

3. _____
_____
_____

Scriptures:
Genesis 2:24
Therefore, a man leaves his father and his mother and clings to his wife, and they become one flesh.

Keeping in mind that difficulties overcoming some challenges may lead to unrealistic expectations, we learned that overcoming unrealistic expectations took mutual agreement and honor. This commitment was critical to being on one accord, and helping us model a behavior for others to follow. We had to be honest with ourselves and the unrealistic expectations we had for each other. As we grew in our relationship and understood each other better, we were able to be more transparent with each other.

What are three things the two of you are willing to do in your marriage to continue to overcome some of the challenges you may be facing in your relationship? *If you are single, what are some challenges you foresee in your future relationship?*

Scriptures: Ephesians 5:25 Husbands, love your wives, just as Christ loved the church and gave himself up for her.

Scriptures: Ephesians 5:33. Each of you, however, should love his wife as himself, and a wife should respect her husband.

HUSBAND

1. _____

2. _____

3. _____

SESSION 1. LOVE & LEAD: YOU

WIFE

1. _____

2. _____

3. _____

God's plan unveiled leadership insights for marriage in Genesis 2:24 that helped us to see His way. Such a plan worked when we followed the blueprint and learned to submit our wills to God's.

Although hard work was required for us to submit to each other and God, we did it. However, submission was harder than it should have been, because we tried marriage our way first. Over time, we recognized His way was better.

What is one thing you know about God's plan for marriage? Write one thing preventing you from implementing God's plan or may prevent you from implementing God's plan in your future relationship. Name one thing you are doing to fulfill God's plan.

HUSBAND

1. KNOW: _____
_____
_____

2. PREVENT: _____
_____
_____

3. DO: _____
_____
_____

WIFE

1. KNOW: _____
_____
_____

2. PREVENT: _____
_____
_____

3. DO: _____
_____
_____

SESSION 1. LOVE & LEAD: YOU

This session is focused on you and your marriage. As you worked through part one by gathering your answers to the thought provoking questions, compare your newly informed thoughts to chapter one's questions. Your reflections will prepare you for part two of this session.

Review Questions from Chapter 1, "Your Spouse is not You: Unrealistic Expectations"

1. **Different viewpoints.** How do you identify, discuss, and come to an understanding of different viewpoints? How do you create the environment to discuss different points? How are you willing to embrace the viewpoints of your spouse without being judgmental?

2. **Miscommunication.** What is your objective when you seek advice from others outside of your marriage? What do you intend to gain? How are you willing to protect the agreements made between you and your spouse regardless of outsiders' opinions?

3. **Money.** What feelings do you attach to money? If there is a difference of opinion on finances, what compromises are you willing to make? If you were to write a 5-year financial plan, what would it be?

REFLECTIONS THOUGHTS	QUESTIONS THOUGHTS

Scriptures: Gen. 1:26–27
Then God said, "Let us make mankind in our image, in our likeness, so that they may rule over the fish in the sea and the birds in the sky, over the livestock and all the wild animals, and over all the creatures that move along the ground." So God created mankind in his own image, in the image of God he created them; male and female he created them.

PART TWO: ACTION STEPS

Session one's actions steps builds on your reflection, focusing on understanding yourself and your partner better. Focusing on each other and reflecting on previous actions may lead to a closer connection between the two of you and God. The following exercises will help with identifying the important pieces you will need to put together. In the following exercises, you will examine yourself, analyze your relationship, and create your future. *If you are single, we invite you to anticipate these things as you complete the exercises.*

Step 1. Understand Yourself

This action step contains three activities: (a) record your voice, (b) smile in the mirror, and (c) write an affirmation. These activities are designed to be done by you. As you complete the activities, reflecting on the results may confirm or change your mind on how you felt about yourself.

A. Record your voice. Speak on something that you are passionate about. As you complete this activity, focus on how you sound and your confidence level when you are speaking. When you listen to the recording, reflect on your level of confidence. Ask someone else to listen to the recording and provide honest feedback. Compare the two responses in Figures 2 and 3. If you are confident, think about what makes you confident when you speak on the topic. If you do not come across as confident, reflect on what is causing you to come across in that manner. Use this activity to focus on you and your ability to convey how you are feeling and how it comes across to others.

|—————————|—————————|—————————|
| Not Confident | Somewhat Confident | Fully Confident |

Figure 2. Your Confidence Level

SESSION 1. LOVE & LEAD: YOU

|————————————|————————————|
Not   Somewhat   Fully
Confident   Confident   Confident

Figure 3. Feedback on Confidence

WHAT MAKES YOU CONFIDENT?

1. _____
_____
_____

2. _____
_____
_____

3. _____
_____
_____

WHAT CAUSES YOU TO *NOT* BE CONFIDENT?

1. _____
_____
_____

2. _____
_____
_____

3. _____
_____
_____

Scriptures:
Ps. 139:13-14
For you created my inmost being; you knit me together in my mother's womb. I praise you because I am fearfully and wonderfully made; your works are wonderful; I know that full well.

What does this say about you? Reflect on how you felt inside and how you came across in audio only. Note your insights as you prepare for the next visual activity.

B. Smile in the mirror. Smiling conveys confidence and makes you more approachable. As you complete this activity, focus on how you feel and look. When you are ready take a picture of your best smile. Next, ask someone else to look at it and provide honest feedback. Compare the two responses in Figures 4 and 5. If you are confident, think about what makes you confident when you look at the picture. If you do not come across as confident, reflect on what is causing you to come across in that manner. Practice smiling in front of the mirror so your smile appears natural. When you smile, people will be drawn to you and more willing to listen to what you have to say.

|—————————|—————————|
Not Confident   Somewhat Confident   Fully Confident

Figure 4. Your Confidence Level

|—————————|—————————|
Not Confident   Somewhat Confident   Fully Confident

Figure 5. Feedback on Confidence

WHAT MAKES YOU CONFIDENT?

1. _____

2. _____

3. _____

Scriptures:
Jeremiah 17:7
But blessed is the one who trusts in the Lord, whose confidence is in him.

SESSION 1. LOVE & LEAD: YOU

WHAT CAUSES YOU TO *NOT* BE CONFIDENT?

1. _____

2. _____

3. _____

What does this say about you? Reflect on how you felt inside and how you were presented via picture. Note your insights as you prepare for the next written task.

C. Write an affirmation. Telling yourself you are confident and successful can work wonders for your mindset. As you complete this activity, focus on positive affirmations to boost your inner confidence so that it can shine outwards. While affirmations alone won't make you the best person, husband or wife, they can inspire you to try your best each day. Use this activity to focus on positive thinking, which can go a long way towards building up your self-confidence and encouraging others.

Scriptures: Proverbs 18:16 A man's gift opens doors for him and brings him before great men.

NAME THINGS YOU LIKE ABOUT YOURSELF.

1. _____

2. _____

3. _____

Example Affirmations:

- Today, I step closer to my purpose in God.
- I will develop my gift, the world needs it.
- I will keep going no matter what, God is with me.

WRITE YOUR AFFIRMATIONS.

Scriptures:
2 Thess. 3:3 But the Lord is faithful. He will establish you and guard you against the evil one.

How does this make you feel? Reflect on how you felt inside, knowing that you are about to build your confidence. Note your insights as you prepare for the next step in your relationship or future relationship.

Through the first action step, you should have a better idea of your strengths and weaknesses and how to improve them. This awareness is key to the next step. Next, you will put the pieces together to see how well they fit and how you can make them fit better.

Step 2. Analyze Your Relationship

In this action step, you will use the same three tasks as above. In this portion, you and your spouse will work through this step together. As a pair, you will look at your strengths and weaknesses. See if the results surprise or confirm your thoughts about your marriage. *If you are single, we invite you to complete these activities with someone close to you who will give you honest feedback as practice for when you are joined with your future partner.*

SESSION 1. LOVE & LEAD: YOU

A. Record your voice. Choose a that ignites passion in both of you when discussed. Record the flow back and forth between each of you regarding the topic. As you complete this activity, focus on how you two sound as a couple when speaking on the selected topic. When you listen to the recording, reflect on your teamwork. Then, ask someone else to listen to the recording and provide honest feedback. Compare the two responses in Figures 6 and 7. If teamwork was evident, think about how well you complete the task. If teamwork is lacking, reflect on what is causing the relationship to suffer. Use this activity to focus on the interaction and the ability to convey your marriage to others.

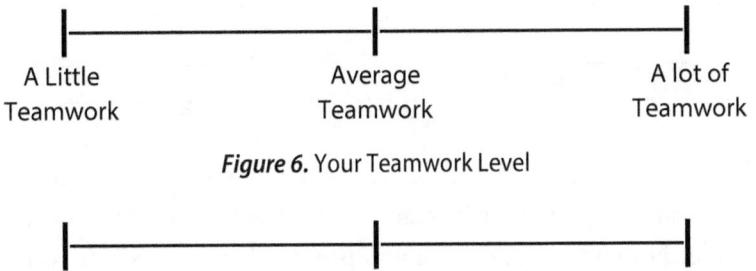

Figure 6. Your Teamwork Level

Figure 7. Feedback on Teamwork

HOW DID YOU KNOW YOU HAD TEAMWORK?

1. _____

2. _____

3. _____

4. _____

HOW DID YOU KNOW YOUR TEAMWORK WAS LACKING?

1. _____

2. _____

3. _____

4. _____

What does this say about your relationship? Reflect on how you felt inside and how your interaction with your partner came across audible. Note your insights as you prepare for the next visual task.

B. Smile in the mirror. As mentioned earlier smiling conveys confidence. This time, look at the confidence between each other rather than one person. Practice smiling in the mirror with your spouse, making it fun. As you complete this activity, focus on how you feel and look with your mate. When you are ready, take a picture of your best smile together. Then, ask someone else to look at it and provide honest feedback. Compare the two responses in Figures 8 and 9. If you are confident with each other, think about what makes a pair confident as you look at the picture. If you do not come across as confident, reflect on what is causing you to come across in that manner. People are drawn to power couples who have confidence in themselves.

Scriptures: Eccl. 4:9 Two are better than one, because they have a good reward for their toil.

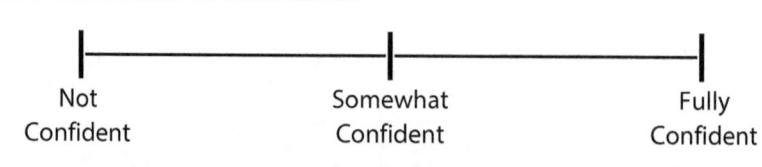

Figure 8. Confidence Level

SESSION 1. LOVE & LEAD: YOU

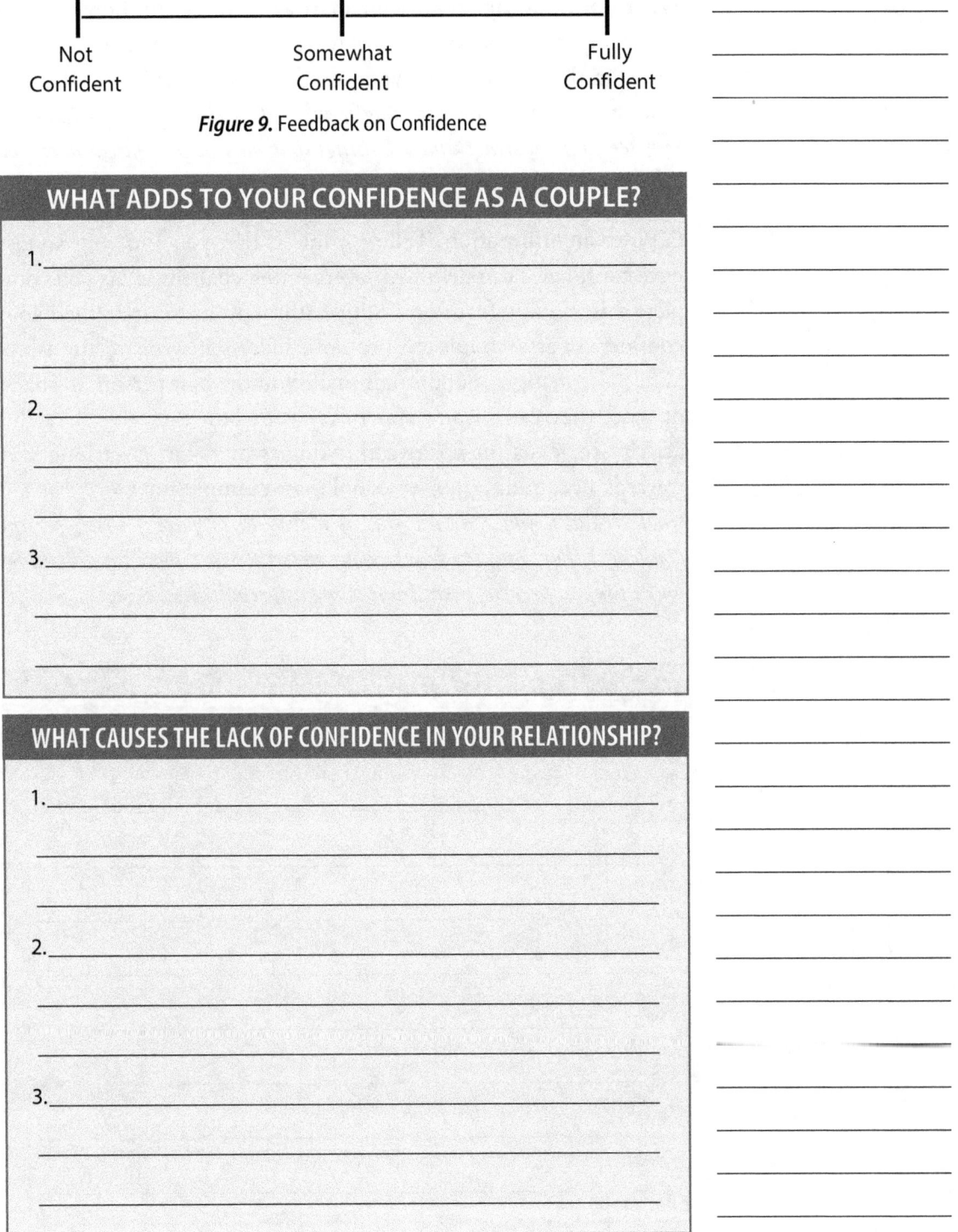

Figure 9. Feedback on Confidence

WHAT ADDS TO YOUR CONFIDENCE AS A COUPLE?

1. _____
   _____
   _____

2. _____
   _____
   _____

3. _____
   _____
   _____

WHAT CAUSES THE LACK OF CONFIDENCE IN YOUR RELATIONSHIP?

1. _____
   _____
   _____

2. _____
   _____
   _____

3. _____
   _____
   _____

What does this say about your marriage? Reflect on how you felt inside and how you and your partner or future partner were presented in the picture. Note your insights as you prepare for the next written activity. *If you are single, what does this say about how you may see your marriage and the things that may be prevented when you are united with your spouse?*

C. Write an affirmation. Telling yourself that you and your spouse have confidence can help with overcoming challenges. As you complete this activity, focus on positive affirmations to strengthen your confidence, as a couple, to promote success in your relationship. While affirmations alone won't make you the best person, husband or wife, they can inspire you to try your best each day. Use this activity to focus on positive thinking, which can go a long way towards becoming a power couple, an example for God. *For our single readers, you may use this as a way to prepare yourself for the challenges that you may face in your marriage and have an advantage on helping to prevent them from being as prevalent.*

NAME THINGS YOU LIKE ABOUT YOUR MARRIAGE
1.
2.
3.

NAME THINGS YOU WANT TO IMPROVE WITH YOUR MARRIAGE

1. _____

2. _____

3. _____

Example Affirmations:

- We are blessed everywhere we go.
- We can achieve more together.
- We are the promises of God.

WRITE YOUR AFFIRMATIONS

How do you feel about your union now? Reflect on how you feel, knowing that you are about to build confidence between the two of you. Note your insights as you build your future. *If you are single, what are some things you were able to identify and how will you use this knowledge to help you overcome in your marriage?*

Through the second action step, you should have a better idea of how to improve your partner's strengths and weaknesses. Building on this awareness is key to the next step. Next, you will visualize where you want to go as a couple in the future.

Step 3. Create Your Future

This action step combines the previous two tasks lessons and looks forward to the future. With the insights gained from you and your partner, how do you envision the next year together. Through confidence and trust, you and your spouse have the necessary tools to develop a road map. Within this step is an activity to develop a road map. You will complete this activity as a way to build your future together. *If you are single, consider how you see your future once you are joined with your spouse and create a tentative road map to be finalized with your future spouse.*

A. Developing a road map. Developing a road map creates a path for your future. It helps declutter the mind, focusing energy towards action. In this activity the two of you will look at five areas of focus for the next year.

1. **Faith.** Envision the both of you growing in the Lord, stronger, wiser, and bolder in the things of God. Would you choose to use a more structured devotional plan or more prayer to grow stronger in your faith?

2. **Family.** Think about how you want to celebrate important days or crave some much-needed quality time like date nights. Does it look like twice a month or once a week? Set aside time on the calendar.

SESSION 1. LOVE & LEAD: YOU

3. **Finances.** Write down your goals. Where do you want to be in a year? For example, paying tithes to God (10% of income), establishing an emergency fund ($1000). For example, paying tithes to God (10% of income), establishing an emergency fund ($1000), and a vacation or retirement fund. Having a financial plan can be beneficial for the future of your relationship.

4. **Fitness.** Imagine your mental and physical goals. Where would you like to be at the end of the year? For instance, would you like to run a half or full marathon or remember the books of the bible or sharpening your faith in God.

Take your ideas for the above four areas and write them down on a piece of paper. At the top you will have all the months from the 1st to the 12th month and on the left-hand side you will have the faith, family, finances, and fitness written down (see Figure 9). After you complete the exercise and are happy with the results, transfer them to your calendar, choosing the dates that work with your schedule. Now you have a working road map for your family.

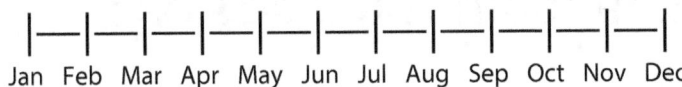

Jan Feb Mar Apr May Jun Jul Aug Sep Oct Nov Dec

Faith

Family

Finance

Fitness

Figure 9. Example of a Working Road map.

Through the third action step, you should have a better idea of how to work towards a brighter future. Your future should be clear; if not, continue to work toward your goals. Note your potential challenges as you begin to work towards your future.

Putting all the three steps together is easier than you think. You have worked on yourself and your relationship, now consider your future. Continue to be transparent with your spouse and lead with love, while trusting God for the increase in your life and marriage. We encourage you to enjoy the journey, the good, the bad, and the ugly.

Closing Prayer

Dear Heavenly Father,

Thank you for your love and kindness. Thank you for your grace and mercy that is new to us every morning. We thank you for reminding us in 2 Corinthians 12:9 that your grace is sufficient for us. We understand that as we continue to abide in you and your word in us John 15:7, we will be victorious. We know that you are love and the love that you have for us is unconditional.

Lord we ask that you continue to strengthen us in love as we continue to grow with each other as a couple. We pray that we can be an example to ourselves and others. We also pray that our journey can be a testament to your glory.

In Jesus' name, Amen!

YOUR THOUGHTS FROM SESSION 1

_____
_____
_____
_____
_____
_____
_____
_____

SESSION 1. LOVE & LEAD: YOU

SESSION 2.
LOVE & LEAD: VALUE

Based on Chapter 2 of *Making Love Work While Leading Your Family*, "Know the Value of Your Spouse: Avoiding the Pitfall of Divorce."

Session's Challenge: Realizing what is worth fighting for with God: defending your marriage and family at all costs.

SELF-REFLECTION

Married Couples: What do you love most about your partner's values and beliefs?

Single Individuals: While reflecting on your relationship history, what values and beliefs attracted you the most?

Opening Prayer

Dear Heavenly Father,
As your dedicated servants, we thank you for allowing us to understand the value of our relationship. Lord help us to continue to grow in love and remember to value each other and respect the other's beliefs.

Lord as we reflect on our relationship, allow us to be willing to compromise and always consider how important our relationship is. Lord help us continue to love one another even through the tough times. Help us to remember 1 Peter 4:8, "Above all, love each other deeply; because love covers over a multitude of sins." Let us remember that we are in this for better or worse, in sickness and health till death do us part.
In Jesus' name, Amen.

NOTES:

Nugget: Completing this session requires learning from your relationship experiences with your spouse and God.

Scriptures: 1st Thessalonians 5:11
Therefore encourage one another and build one another up, just as you and doing.

Zacardi Cortez "You Don't Know."

PART ONE: REFLECTION

Our problems that came along with avoiding divorce were difficult, as depicted in Figure 10. With God's answers, we fought for our marriage in Chapter 2. We gained strength in God, transforming ourselves into victors in Christ instead of victims of life. We did not value each other. We failed to respect the others experiences and wanted to force our thoughts and beliefs on each other. Unfortunately, our interaction lead to a lack of love. We loved each other, but we were not in-love with each other.

Scriptures:
Hebrews 3:13
But exhort one another every day, as long as it is called "today," so that none of you may be hardened by the deceitfulness of sin.

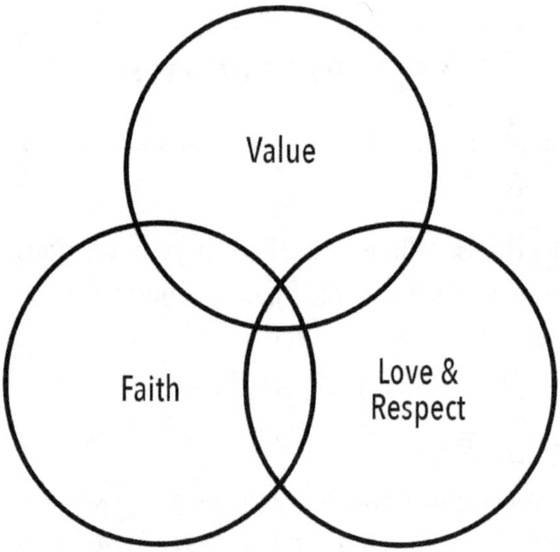

Figure 10. Chapter 2's central themes with our problems, lessons, and insights.

Our marriage lessons highlighted that God was the key. Not only was God the focal point for valuing our spouse, He also helped us become unified. This resolve assisted us with preventing divorce.

Valuing your spouse is a significant part of establishing a healthy marriage. Reflect on the things that you value about your spouse. *List the top three things that you value in a future partner if you're single.*

HUSBAND

1. _____

2. _____

3. _____

WIFE

1. _____

2. _____

3. _____

Identify three things that you are willing to do to make sure that your spouse understands how much you value and appreciate him or her. *If you are single, list three things you are willing to make sure you do so that your future spouse knows you appreciate him or her.*

HUSBAND

1. _____
_____
_____

2. _____
_____
_____

3. _____
_____
_____

WIFE

1. _____
_____
_____

2. _____
_____
_____

3. _____
_____
_____

Scripture: Proverbs 3:5-6 Trust in the Lord with all your heart, and don not rely on your own insight. In all your ways acknowledge him, and he will make straight your path.

As we reflected on leadership insights, we learned to trust God with our lives. King David also taught us that fighting, seeking and pursuing God helped with our building blocks of faith, as we moved towards greater things.

SESSION 2. LOVE & LEAD: VALUE

This session provides an opportunity for you to discover value in your marriage. As you gather answers in part one, you can begin to compare them to questions from Chapter 2. Your reflections will prepare you for part two of this session.

Review Questions from Chapter 2, "Know the Value of Your Spouse: Avoiding the Pitfall of Divorce."

1. **Valuing each other.** How do you identify your value and communicate it to each other? How do you create an environment to discuss each other's strengths and weaknesses? In what ways are you willing to support your spouse to show that you value them without being critical?

2. **Faith.** What do you expect from God when you seek Him for answers to your problems? How do you build a relationship with Him to strengthen your faith? In what ways are you willing to wait on God to answer your prayers when you are running out of time?

3. **Love and Respect.** What feelings do you attach to love and respect? How do you identify your love and respect language and communicate it to each other? If you were to write a plan on how to love and respect your spouse, what would it be?

REFLECTIONS THOUGHTS	QUESTIONS THOUGHTS

PART TWO: ACTION STEPS

Knowing the value of your spouse or significant other is important when it comes to the way you treat him or her and the way your partner treats you. We all desire to be respected and appreciated. However, in order to truly value someone else, you have to value and understand yourself. You have to be willing to connect with your partner and truly understand him or her for who they are as a person. Finally, you have to see that person as a part of your future. It is with great consideration that we are presenting you with activities that you can take part in to help you explore how much you value your loved one.

Step 1. Understand Yourself

This action step contains three activities: (a) tell yourself that you love yourself three times while looking in the mirror, (b) identify three things you most value about yourself, and (c) start a journal reflecting on your thoughts about yourself daily. These activities are designed to be done by you. As you complete the activities please reflect on the results, which may confirm or change your mind on how you felt about yourself.

A. Express your admiration for yourself. Tell yourself "I love you" at least three times while looking at yourself in the mirror. As you do this, focus on your voice and how it sounds to hear you tell yourself how much you love you. As you complete this activity, keep in mind that you are valuable, and it is important for you to truly love yourself before you can love your partner with every part of you.

Reflect on how you felt inside, and do you truly value yourself when you said those words or was it hard to hear you are worthy. Note your insights as you prepare for the next written task.

B. Know your worth. Identify three things that you most value about yourself. Acknowledge your gifts and talents. Remember never to minimize the skills that you have.

Scriptures: Psalms 139:14 I praise you, for I am fearfully and wonderfully made. Wonderful are your works; that I know very well.

SESSION 2. LOVE & LEAD: VALUE

NAME THINGS YOU VALUE ABOUT YOURSELF.

1. _____
2. _____
3. _____

NAME SOME OF YOUR GIFTS GIVEN BY GOD.

1. _____
2. _____
3. _____

NAME SOME GIFTS THAT WERE DEVELOPED INTO TALENTS.

1. _____
2. _____
3. _____

Did you recognize that you have God-given gifts or that you have developed some of them? Reflect on your realization that you used or did not use what God has given you. Note your insights as you prepare for the next written task.

C. Write in a Journal. Start a daily journal and write a quick note about what you experienced throughout your day. Write down how you responded to various situations and even how others responded to you. The key is to reflect on your reactions to situations that you experienced throughout the day. After about a month, look at what you wrote at the beginning of the previous month and reflect on what you wrote. Continue this exercise and try not to review what you wrote until at least a month after you began writing that set of entries.

What did you notice from month-to-month, are you seeing patterns? Reflect on the patterns, knowing that you will address them by becoming better. Note your insights as you prepare for the next step in your relationship.

Through the first action step, you should have a better idea of your strengths and weaknesses and how to improve them, by building confidence using ears, eyes, and mind. This awareness is key to the next step. Next, you will put the pieces together to see how well they fit and how you can make them fit better.

Step 2. Analyze Your Commitment

In this action step, you will use the same three tasks as above. The difference here is, you and your spouse will work through this step together. As a couple, you will look at your strengths and weaknesses. See if the results surprise or confirm your thoughts about your marriage. *If you are single, please consider the things that you will apply once you are joined with your spouse as you work through this section.*

A. Express your admiration for your partner. Tell your partner "I love you" at least three times throughout the day while looking him or her in the eyes. As you do this, focus on your loved one's response and the emotion that he or she displays. As you complete this activity, keep in mind how valuable your partner truly is, and the importance of loving him or her completely for you to truly advance in your relationship while enhancing the value that you place on your significant other.

What does this say about your relationship? Reflect on how your marriage grew closer or apart, from the activity. Note your insights as you prepare for the next written task.

B. Know your worth. Share the things that you value most about each other. After the other person has shared their thoughts and feelings, let them know that you appreciate this action. Following one partner sharing, the other will do the same. As before, once the second partner shares, the other should express genuine appreciation for sharing their thoughts. This activity is designed to help you understand yourself from a different person's point of view. It is meant to emphasize the value that your significant other sees in you and the value that you see in him/her.

WHAT ARE THREE WAYS I VALUE MY HUSBAND?

1. _____
_____
_____

2. _____
_____
_____

3. _____
_____
_____

WHAT ARE THREE WAYS I VALUE MY WIFE?

1. _____
   _____
   _____

2. _____
   _____
   _____

3. _____
   _____
   _____

What does this say about your marriage or indicate for your future marriage? Reflect on how you and your partner was on the same page or not, was this a surprise? Note your insights as you prepare for the next written activity.

C. Write in a journal. Start a daily journal and a least write a quick note about your interaction with your partner throughout the day. Write down how you responded to various situations and how your significant other responded to you. The key is to reflect on your partner's reactions to situations that you two experienced together throughout the day. After about a month, look at what you wrote at the beginning of the previous month and reflect on what you wrote. Continue this exercise and try not to review what you wrote until at least a month after you began writing that set of entries.

Building on this awareness is key to the next step. How do you feel about your relationship, now? Reflect on how you feel, knowing that you are about to build confidence between you. Note your insights as you build your future.

Through the second action step, you should have a better idea of how to improve the strengths and weaknesses in your relationship. Next, you will visualize where you want to go as couple in the future.

Step 3. Create Your Future

This action step combines the previous two steps and looks forward to the future. With the insights gained from the yourself and your significant other, how do you envision the next year together. Through confidence and trust, you and your spouse have the necessary tools to pave a road forward. This step contains an activity, developing a vision board. Together, you will do this activity as a way to build your future together.

A. Create a Vision Board. Create a Vision Board for your future as a couple. You have options to use magazine pictures, newspapers, and other sources of words and pictures. You may arrange the pictures and words in the form of a collage. Please note, it can be organized however you like. Some people like to have things in chronological order, while others may present it as a "true" collage. For specific ideas, you can search vision boards on Google or Pinterest.

Through the third action step, you should have a better idea of how to work towards a brighter future. Your future should be clearer, if not continue to refine. Note your potential challenges as you begin to work towards the completion of your vision board.

Putting all the three steps together is easier than you think. You have worked on your relationship, now it is time to work towards your future. Continue to be transparent with your spouse and lead with love, while trusting God for the increase. We encourage you to enjoy the journey, the good, the bad, and the ugly.

Scriptures:
Jeremiah 29:11
For surely I know the plans I have for you, says the Lord, plans for your welfare and not for harm, to give you a future with hope.

Closing Prayer

Heavenly Father,
Thank you for allowing us to find the comfort in knowing that we can join our values and beliefs together as we work to strengthen our bond in this partnership. Help us to trust in you so we can continue to honor each other as individuals.

Allow our love to continue to grow stronger as we join our values and beliefs together to set an example for our children and grandchildren. As we lean on Proverbs 3:5, continue to lead and guide us to all understanding according to your will.
In Jesus' name, Amen

YOUR THOUGHTS FROM SESSION 2

SESSION 2. LOVE & LEAD: VALUE

SESSION 3.
LOVE & LEAD: COMMUNICATION

Based on Chapter 3 of *Making Love Work While Leading Your Family*, "Communication is Key: Focusing on the Non-Verbal."

Session's Challenge: Discovering how to cut through the noise to connect with your spouse and align with God.

SELF-REFLECTION

Married Couples: How did you and your spouse communicate in the beginning of your relationship?

Singles: What are some key things that you focus on when it comes to communicating with a potential mate?

Opening Prayer

Dear Heavenly Father,
In your word, you say a soft answer turneth away wrath, but grievous words stir up anger (Proverbs 15:1). Lord help us to reflect on our communication and work towards developing even better ways to communicate with each other. Help us to understand how the other communicates, and genuinely learn how to listen to our partner.

As we move forward, help us to understand the significance of non-verbal communication and the impact that it has on our partner. Keep us focused on the things that are important to help continue to build a successful relationship where communication is quintessential concerning our relationship.
In Jesus name, Amen.

NOTES

Nugget: Completing this session requires openness and willingness to assess your level of communication.

Scriptures: Proverbs 15:1
A soft answer turns away wrath, but grievous words stir up anger.

Marvin Sapp
"Listen"

PART ONE: REFLECTION

Chapter 3 detailed our lack of success with non-verbal communication as problems were highlighted in Figure 11. In our season of rest, the Word of God challenged us to stop being petty. In turn, we started loving each other which required listening.

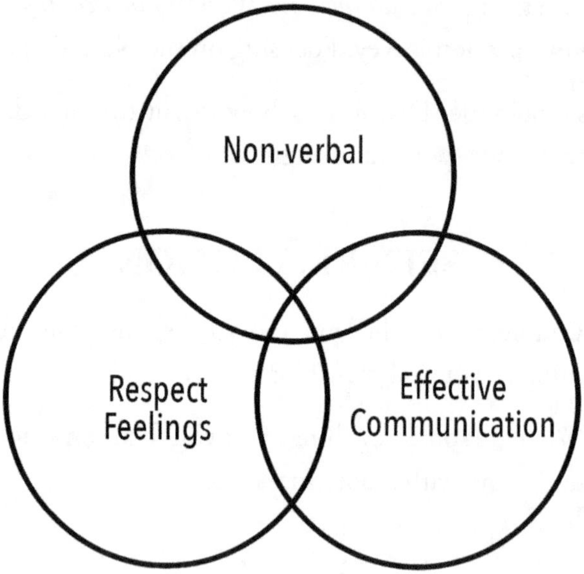

Scriptures: Proverbs 18:4 The words of the mouth are deep waters; the fountain of wisdom is a gushing stream.

Figure 11. Chapter 3's central themes with our problems, lessons, and insights.

Our challenges with non-verbal communication interfered with the ability to effectively communicate with each other. Since we did not build upon good communication in the beginning, we lacked respect for the other because we did not feel as though the other was being heard.

Consider your relationship or what you look for in a relationship as it relates to communication. Address three areas of your communication that needs to be improved. *We encourage singles to reflect on previous relationships or how you would like to see communication between you and your future spouse.*

SESSION 3. LOVE & LEAD: COMMUNICATION

WIFE
1. _____
_____
_____
2. _____
_____
_____
3. _____
_____

Scriptures: Hebrews 5:33 Each of you, however, should love his wife as himself, and a wife should respect her husband.

Review Questions from Chapter 3, "Communication Is Key: Focusing on the Non-Verbal."

1. **Identifying the Non-Verbal Cues.** How do you communicate with your spouse non-verbally? What are some of the challenges that you have faced in your relationship because of non-verbal communication? How would you say the challenges that you had with your spouse with non-verbal communication improved your ability to communicate?

HUSBAND

1. _____
_____
_____

2. _____
_____
_____

3. _____
_____
_____

1. **Respecting Each Other's Feelings When Communicating.** How do you deal with managing conflict? In what ways would you say you have disregarded your spouse's feelings when communicating? What have you learned as a result of your spouse's response when he / she felt undervalued regarding his / her feelings?

2. **Building Effective Communication.** How would you define effective communication in your marriage? What are some steps that you can take to ensure that you effectively communicate with your spouse? What is one thing that you are willing to commit to help increase effective communication within your marriage?

REFLECTIONS THOUGHTS	QUESTIONS THOUGHTS

PART TWO: ACTION STEPS

As we work to build communication within our relationships, it can be a challenge to identify some of the areas in which we may fall short. Taking time to reflect and complete activities to highlight some of the things that we may take for granted when communicating with our partner can help highlight some of the areas where work may be needed. We are excited to provide you with some examples of exercises that you can take part in with your partner to pinpoint some of the areas that may need work. We hope these things can help improve communication within your relationship.

Step 1. Understand Yourself

This action step contains three activities: (a) pay more attention, (b) identify your non-verbal cues, and (c) commit to making a change. These activities are designed to be done by you. As you complete the activities, please reflect on the results that may confirm or change your mind on how you felt about yourself.

Scriptures: Proverbs 15:4 A gentle tongue is a tree of life, but perverseness in it breaks the spirit.

A. Pay more attention to non-verbals. Pay more attention to the way you communicate. Try focusing on the incidents where challenges with communication take place; take inventory of how you respond. As you complete this activity, try to focus on no more than two non-verbal responses at a time so you are able to pinpoint them and really focus on making sure you keep in mind how you feel when your partner is non-verbally aggressive towards you.

TWO NON-VERBAL RESPONSES FOR DEALING WITH AGGRESSION

1. _____

_____

_____

_____

2. _____

_____

_____

_____

B. Identify your verbal cues. Consider how you communicate verbally when you and your significant other have a disagreement. Think about what you can do to improve your verbal communication. Try to focus on taking into consideration how it makes you feel when your significant other says hurtful things to you.

SESSION 3. LOVE & LEAD: COMMUNICATION

TWO NON-VERBAL RESPONSES FOR DEALING WITH DISAGREEMENT

1. _____

2. _____

C. Commit to making a change. Once you have identified the non-verbal and verbal communication that may be offensive to your partner or your future partner, commit to making a change. Identify at least two of each type to improve and take to time be mindful of how often you respond in an aggressive manner both verbally and non-verbally. Remember, as you are working through this process, always consider how you feel when your significant other responds aggressively in a non-verbal and verbal manner towards you.

Scriptures: James 1:2-3 My brothers and sisters, whenever you face trials of any kind, consider it nothing but joy, because you know that the testing of your faith produces endurance.

WAYS TO IMPROVE YOUR NON-VERBAL COMMUNICATION

1. _____

2. _____

Through the first action step, you should have a better idea of your communication strengths and weaknesses and how to improve them, by improving your attention to detail. This awareness is key to the next step and strengthening your relationship.

Step 2. Analyze Your Interaction

In this action step, you will use the same three tasks as above. The difference here is, you and your spouse will work through this step together. As a couple, you will look at your strengths and weaknesses. See if the results surprise or confirm your thoughts about your marriage. *If you are single, consider your methods of communication and how you would like to improve as you prepare yourself for your future spouse.*

A. Pay more attention to non-verbals. Pay more attention to the way you communicate. Try focusing on the incidents where challenges with communication take place, take inventory of how you respond. As you complete this activity, try to focus on no more than two non-verbal responses at a time so you are able to pinpoint them and really focus on making sure you keep in mind how your partner feels when you are non-verbally aggressive towards him or her. Take time to ask your partner how he or she feels.

TWO NON-VERBAL RESPONSES
1. _____
_____
_____
2. _____
_____
_____

B. Identify non-verbal cues. Consider how you communicate non-verbally when you and your significant other have a disagreement. Think about what you can do to improve your non-verbal communication. Try to focus on taking into consideration how it makes your partner feel when you do hurtful things towards him or her. Remember to ask him or her how it makes them feel to help you identify the non-verbal cues.

> **TWO NON-VERBAL RESPONSES FOR DEALING WITH DISAGREEMENT**
>
> 1. _____
> _____
> _____
> _____
>
> 2. _____
> _____
> _____
> _____

C. Commit to making a change. Once you have identified your non-verbal and verbal communication that may be offensive to your partner, commit to making a change. Identify at least two of each type to improve and take to time be mindful of how often you respond in an aggressive manner both verbally and non-verbally. Remember, as you are working through this process, always consider how your significant other feels when each of you respond aggressively in a non-verbal and verbal manner. It is imperative that you and your loved one work together to make the change needed.

> **WAYS TO IMPROVE YOUR NON-VERBAL COMMUNICATION**
>
> 1. _____
> _____
> _____
> _____
>
> 2. _____
> _____
> _____
> _____

How do you feel about your relationship now? Reflect on how you feel, knowing that you are continuing to develop effective communication skills. Note your insights as you build your future.

Through the second action step, you should have a better idea of how to improve your strengths and weaknesses as a couple. Building on this awareness is key to the next step. Next, you will visualize how you will build on your communication skills in the future.

Step 3. Create Your Future

This action step combines the previous two tasks lessons and looks forward to the future. With the insights gained from the yourself and your spouse, and as you progress in your relationship, continue to assess how you communicate with each other. Making communication a priority can not only help improve how you interact with one another, but it will improve the overall quality of your relationship. *If you are single, based on previous relationships, consider how you would like to communicate with your future spouse.*

SESSION 3. LOVE & LEAD: COMMUNICATION

A. Review communication. Look at the history of you and your spouses' communication. Practice identifying signals and codes for each other when you get to the point that you feel as though the you need to take a break from a "heated" conversation. We invite you to come up with code words or non-verbal gestures to let the other know that you are reaching your "breaking point." Making it a priority to do these simple things can help decrease conflict and increase the understand of your partners method of communication. Better communication opens up healthier dialogue once you both are ready to express yourselves again.

Through the third action step, you should have a better idea of how work towards a healthier future through communication. Working with your partner on effective communication is essential in any relationship.

Putting all the three steps together is easier than you think. You have worked on yourself and your relationship. Now it is important that you consider your future. Continue to communicate with your partner and learn the most effective ways to express yourselves with each other. We hope that you enjoy the life that you are building together and remain open.

Closing Prayer

Heavenly Father,
When we find ourselves having difficultly communicating, help us communicate with you. Dear Lord, teach us how to listen to one another and talk to each other not past each other. Help us to be connected on a higher level so that we can remember why we chose each other.

Lord help us remember to always use wisdom when we speak to one another. We desire to increase our communication so that we can be an example to others of what a strong relationship built on communication should be. We thank you, Lord for your love and protection over our lives. In Jesus' name we pray.
Thank God, Amen.

YOUR THOUGHTS FROM SESSION 3

_____
_____
_____
_____
_____
_____
_____
_____
_____

SESSION 3. LOVE & LEAD: COMMUNICATION

SESSION 4.
LOVE & LEAD: CONFLICT

Based on Chapter 4 of *Making Love Work While Leading Your Family*, "Conflict is Good: Healthy Ways to Deal with Conflict."

Session's Challenge: Recognizing how to resolve conflict with your spouse, strengthening the marriage for the long haul.

SELF-REFLECTION

Married Couples: How did you handle conflict at the beginning of your relationship?

Singles: What are some things that you consider when thinking about how to handle conflict in a relationship?

Opening Prayer

Dear Heavenly Father,
We thank you for helping us understand how we learn from each other even in the midst of conflict. Help lead and guide us as we navigate the challenges within our relationship. As we face difficulties and our faith is tried, help us to remember that faith builds patience-James 1:2-3.

As we continue to learn from our experiences, allow us to grow deeper in love and our relationship continue to be strengthened. In the tough times, help us to remember Philippians 4:13, "I can do all things through Christ who strengthens me." Continue to open our hearts to be receptive to one another so that we can, in turn, use the trials that we have overcome with your strength to help others.
In Jesus' name. Amen.

NOTES

Nugget: Completing this session requires self-regulation.

Scriptures: Ephesians 4:26-27
Be ye angry, and sin not: let not the sun go down upon your wrath: Neither give place to the devil.

Marvin Sapp "He Saw the Best in Me"

PART ONE: REFLECTION

Chapter 4 highlighted our problems with not listening, resulting in conflict. The lack of attention resulted in problems, as shown in Figure 12. Facing our inability to stay properly balanced and our inability to manage our obligations, the Holy Spirit illuminated ways for us the put our family first and find happiness God's way.

Scriptures: Ephesians 4:31-32
Put away from you all bitterness and wrath and anger and wrangling and slander, together with all malice, and be kind to one another, tenderhearted, forgiving one another, as God in Christ has forgiven you.

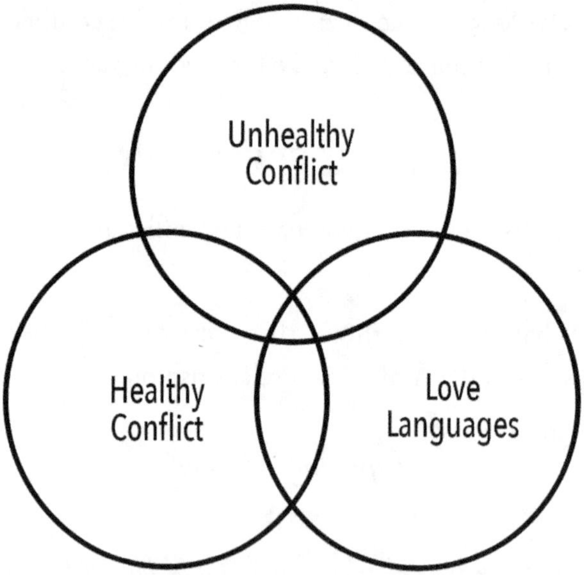

Figure 12. Chapter 4's central themes with our problems, lessons, and insights.

We all experience conflict in our relationships. Sometimes the conflict is unhealthy. When we have a disagreement and both or one of the individuals is extremely upset to the point of no reasoning, that can turn into a situation where unhealthy conflict may arise. However, there are aspects of conflict that are good. When you and your partner may have a disagreement, but you can rationally come to a compromise and resolve the issue in a healthy manner there is more potential for growth within the relationship.

SESSION 4. LOVE & LEAD: CONFLICT

Through experiencing all forms of conflict, an essential aspect of getting through the challenges is that you learn how to deal with your partner in tense situations. Furthermore, the ability to identify and understand his or her love language becomes more prevalent.

Consider the various challenges encountered throughout your relationship. Think of three specific instances where there was conflict within your relationship. What are some things that you would have done differently? List some things that you can say that you learned about your spouse from the experiences. *If you're single, consider your past friendships or relationships where you had to navigate conflict, how did you do it and did you learn anything?*

HUSBAND
1.
2.
3.

Scriptures: Proverbs 15:18
Those who are hot-tempered stir up strife, but those who are slow to anger calm contention.

WIFE
1. _____   _____   _____   2. _____   _____   _____   3. _____   _____   _____

As we progressed in our marriage, we were unaware of how to deal with conflict. We often found ourselves having conflicts with one another and it led more towards unhealthy conflict. Upon reflection, we realized the healthy conflicts we had ended up turning into an argument because we did not effectively communicate. However, when we began to understand each other's love language, it was easier to decipher between healthy and unhealthy conflict and resolve any disagreements.

Our marriage lessons included description of how we dealt with conflict and how learned to build deep trust through understanding your spouse's love language. Apostle Paul's leadership insights urged us that it was possible to defend yourself in Chapter 4, highlighting that God's track record in our life provided us with ability to deal with conflict.

This session deals with conflict and your ability to respond in a healthy manner with your spouse. As you work through your responses from part one, remember to build on your thoughts. Such effort will prepare you for part two of this session.

SESSION 4. LOVE & LEAD: CONFLICT

Review Questions from Chapter 4, "Conflict is Good: Healthy Ways to Deal with Conflict."

1. **Unhealthy ways to deal with conflict.** When you reflect on your marriage, what are some unhealthy ways that you and your spouse deal with conflict? What are some things that you noticed in yourself when the conflict was not managed in a healthy way? What are some things that you noticed in your spouse when the conflict was not resolved in a constructive manner?

2. **Healthy conflict resolution.** How have you been able to improve your marriage by handling conflict in a healthy way? What are some things that you may have done differently to improve the conflict resolution even more? If you could help your spouse understand how he / she has helped with your ability to resolve conflict in your marriage, what would you say to him / her?

3. **Understanding love languages.** What is your love language? How can you apply the knowledge of your love language to improving your relationship with your spouse? What would you say your spouse's love language is and why?

REFLECTIONS THOUGHTS	QUESTIONS THOUGHTS

PART TWO: ACTION STEPS

Sometimes we underestimate the impact that conflict can have on our relationship. However, we tend to overlook the benefit of it. Considering conflict is not always such a bad thing, we have included some activities that well help identify some of the experiences that lead to conflict along with how each of you, as individuals, deal with conflict internally and externally. We also understand the importance of how planning for your future together can help you maneuver through some of the conflicts that you may have. Planning can also help you to see that the future you have together is worth fighting through the challenges, at a given moment, to reach the goals that the two of you have set for your future together.

Step 1. Understand Yourself

This action step contains three activities: (a) assessing healthy conflict, (b) working towards understanding unhealthy conflict, and (c) identify the love languages. These activities are designed to be done by you. *If you are single reflect on past relationships and think about how you dealt with conflicts.* As you complete the activities please reflect on the results that may confirm or change your mind on how you felt about yourself.

A. Assessing healthy conflict. Consider how you respond to your spouse when you have healthy conflict. Keep in mind those conflicts where you are able to agree to disagree. In those instances, think about the dynamics of the conversation. Also consider your mindset. During your next healthy conflict with your spouse, pay attention to the interaction and your response to your spouse. As you think through those things, consider trying to apply those actions when you are in an argument with your spouse, which would often lead to an unhealthy conflict.

Scriptures:
1st Peter 3:8 Finally, be ye all of one mind, having compassion one of another, love as brethren, be pitiful, be courteous:

SESSION 4. LOVE & LEAD: CONFLICT

B. Working towards understanding unhealthy conflict. Look at yourself and identify things that you would like to change related to your response when dealing with conflict in your relationship. Think about a recent disagreement you had with your partner. What are some things you realize you could have done differently to help prevent the situation from escalating to the point of an argument? Try to keep the things you identified in mind to help you avoid high levels of frustration during the next disagreement with you partner.

C. Identifying love languages. Think about the actions that make you happy when you are the receiver. Focus on your love language and how you translate that when interacting with your partner. Think about how it makes you feel when you receive the various actions.

How does this make you feel? Reflect on how you are working towards resolving conflict. Note your insights as you prepare for the next step in your relationship.

When addressing the first action step, you should have a better insight surrounding your strengths and weaknesses and how to improve them by reflecting on the various levels of conflict that may occur in your relationship. This awareness is key to the next step. Next, you will put the pieces together to see how well they fit and how you can make them fit better.

Step 2. Analyze Your Relationship

In this action step, you will use the same three tasks as above. The difference here is you and your partner will work through this step together. As a couple, you will look at your strengths and weaknesses. *If you are single, consider doing these activities with someone you trust and has your best interest at heart.* See if the results surprise or confirm your thoughts about your marriage.

A. Accessing healthy conflict. Consider how you respond to your spouse or significant other when you have healthy conflict; those conflicts where you are able to agree to disagree. In those instances, think about the dynamics of the conversation. Be sure to also consider your mindset. During your next healthy conflict with your loved one, pay attention to the interaction and your response. As you think through those things, consider trying to apply those actions when you are in an argument with your spouse that would often lead to an unhealthy conflict.

B. Working towards understanding unhealthy conflict. Share them with your significant other. After sharing your thoughts with your partner, have him/ her respond to your assessment of yourself and offer their perception. Please be open minded when completing this exercise and focus on receiving feedback from your spouse and avoid becoming defensive. Please remember, the purpose of this exercise is to get your perspective on yourself and for your spouse to share his or her thoughts.

C. Identify your love language. Think about the actions that make you happy when you are the receiver. Focus on your love language and how you translate it when interacting with your partner. Think about how it makes you feel when you receive the various actions.

How do you feel about your relationship now? Reflect on how you feel, keeping in mind the importance of working through the challenges the two of you have as a couple as it relates to working through conflict. Focus your insights as you consider the path for your future.

Through the second action step, you should have a better idea of how to improve your strengths and weaknesses. Building on this awareness is key to the next step. Next, you will visualize where you want to go as couple in the future.

Step 3. Create Your Future

This action step combines the previous two tasks lessons and looks forward to the future. With the insights gained from the yourself and partner, how do you envision the next year together. Through confidence and trust, you have the necessary tools to develop a road map. This step contains an activity requiring the developing of a road map. Together, you will do this activity as a way to build your future together. *If you are single, we invite you to consider where you would like to be when you are untied with your spouse.*

A. Future goals—Road map. Where do you want to be in your relationship 5 years from now? After you establish the 5-year outlook, look at where you would like to be 10 years from now. We invite you to really look at your goals as it relates to where you are now in your relationship. Make sure you consider the additional steps you need to take to realistically reach the goals that you set for yourselves.

Through the third action step, you should have a better idea of how work towards a brighter future. Your future should be clearer, if not continue to refine. Note your potential challenges as you begin to work towards your future.

Putting all the three steps together is easier than you think. You have worked on yourself, your union, and now your future. Continue to be transparent with your spouse and lead with love, while trusting God for the increase. We encourage to enjoy the journey, the good, the bad, and the ugly.

Scriptures: Proverbs 29:18 Where there is no vision, the people perish.

Closing Prayer

Father God,
We pray that your blood covers us and protects us from all hurt, harm, or danger. We are asking that you continue to give us peace within our relationship. When trials come, give us insight on how to handle them in a calm manner. We want to be pleasing in your sight.

Lord continue to help us to realize that we should become angry and sin not. We pray that we always remember not to go to bed angry and avoid allowing the sun to go down on our wrath. Ephesians 4:26. In Jesus' name we pray, Amen.

YOUR THOUGHTS FROM SESSION 4

_____
_____
_____
_____
_____
_____
_____
_____
_____
_____

SESSION 4. LOVE & LEAD: CONFLICT

SESSION 5.
LOVE & LEAD: INTIMACY

Based on Chapter 5 of *Making Love Work While Leading Your Family*, "Making Love Count: Intimacy."

Session's Challenge: Choosing to honor your spouse in search of true intimacy.

SELF-REFLECTION

Married Couples: What were some of the things that you did in the beginning of your marriage to become comfortable with each other as it relates to intimacy?

Opening Prayer

Dear Heavenly Father,
Thank you for giving us each other. As written in Proverbs 18:22, "He who finds a wife finds a good thing and obtain favor in the Lord." As we continue in our relationship, help us to understand the importance of connecting intimately. Give us wisdom on how to show each other affection even when we don't feel like it. Help us to remember why we feel in love and how important it is for us to continue to establish closeness within our relationship

In your word, Hebrews 13:4 acknowledges that "the marriage bed is undefiled." As we continue to reflect on what intimacy is and how to continue to develop it within our relationship, please help us to remember the significance of what it is to be in love and maintain true passion for one another.

NOTES

 Nugget: Completing this session requires vulnerability with between you and your spouse.

_____

_____

 Scriptures: Matthew 9:4-6 And he answered and said unto them, Have ye not read, that he which made [them] at the beginning made them male and female. And said, For this cause shall a man leave his father and mother and cleave to his wife: and they twain shall be one flesh? Wherefore they are no more twain but one flesh. What therefore God hath joined together, let not man put asunder.

_____

_____

_____

♪ MUSIC Maurette Brown Clark "The One He Kept for Me"

Allow our connection to be more intense each time we share intimate time together.
In Jesus' name, Amen!

PART ONE: REFLECTION

The struggle we had with intimacy caused problems when it came to honoring each other as king and queen. We failed to make time for each other, did not focus on making love, and were not motivated to spicing up our love life. See Figure 13. In the lowest point in our marriage, we were not providing the example we established in Chapter 5 of our book. However, upon the completion of hard work and long-suffering, God swiftly transitioned us from glorified roommates to actively honoring each other as king and queen.

Scriptures:
Genesis 2:18
It is not good for man to be alone; I will make a fitting helper for him.

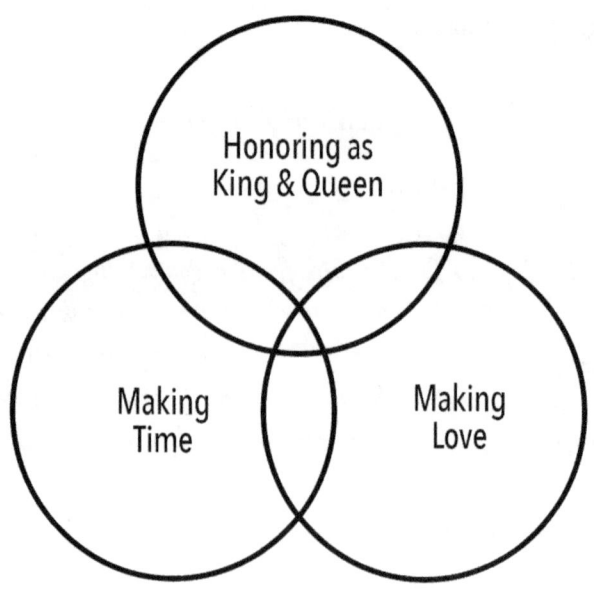

Figure 13. Chapter 5's central themes with our problems, lessons, and insights.

SESSION 5. LOVE & LEAD: INTIMACY

We detailed in our marriage lessons that making love count goes beyond the physical connection. It also deals with the mind and soul.

In our leadership insights, Abraham and Sarah showed us how to have an intimate relationship with our spouse and a deeper connection with God, potentially leading to a generational blessing.

This session deals with conflict and your ability to response in a healthy manner with your spouse. As you work through your responses from part one, remember to build on your thoughts that will help answer questions from chapter four. Such effort will prepare you for part two of this session.

Scriptures: Proverbs 18:22 He who found a wife has found happiness.

Review Questions from Chapter 5, "Making Love Count: Intimacy."

1. **Honoring each other as king and queen.** How have situations from the past limited your ability to honor each other as king and queen? What are some things that you have done to work on building genuine respect for one another? How are you willing to move forward in your marriage to build upon mutual respect between you and your spouse?

Scriptures: Daniel 4:3 How great [are] his signs. And how mighty [are] his wonders. His kingdom [is] from generation to generation.

2. **Making time for each other.** Where are some of your favorite places to go as a couple? What are some of the things that you notice about your marriage when you spend quality time away with your spouse? What are some of your goals surrounding making time for each other?

3. **Making love and spicing up your love life.** How often do you relate intimacy to sex or physical contact? What are some things your spouse can do to build upon the emotional connection that enhances the physical intimacy? What are some things you feel your spouse needs to increase physical intimacy?

REFLECTIONS THOUGHTS	QUESTIONS THOUGHTS

PART TWO: ACTION STEPS

 Scriptures: 1st Corinthians 14:4-8

Love is patient, love is kind, it does not envy, it does not boast, it is not proud. It does not dishonor others, it is not self-seeking, it is not easily angered, it keeps no record of wrongs. Love does not delight in evil but rejoices with the truth. It always protects, always trusts, always hopes, always perseveres. Love never fails.

Making love expands beyond physical contact with your spouse. Making love involves true intimacy. Many people confuse intimacy and making love with the physical act of sexual intercourse. However, becoming one with your spouse involves getting to know him or her through effective communication, spending quality time with each other, and seeing each other in the other's future. We are overjoyed to share activities with you that can help you examine the quality of your relationship and how intimate you truly are with your spouse. Through healthy evaluation, the value of your relationship will be made clear to each of you and the level of true intimacy will intensify. As the intimacy intensifies, there will likely be more passion when you are physically intimate with your spouse.

Step 1. Understand Yourself

This action step contains three activities: (a) honor yourself, (b) make time for yourself, and (c) pamper yourself. These activities are designed to be done by you, for you. As you complete the activities, please reflect on the results, which may confirm or change your mind on how you feel about yourself.

A. Honor yourself. Be confident in who you are as a person. Make sure you know your worth in the relationship. Think of something that you have contributed to the relationship that you are proud of. Tell yourself that you are proud of yourself and acknowledge your contribution to the relationship and identify how it has helped make it better.

B. Make time for yourself. Sometimes you have to take time for yourself. Many times, this includes spending time with friends away from your spouse. Taking time to interact with others who are close to you can be relaxing and rejuvenating, which will help you give more of yourself to your spouse. Take time to plan an outing with someone with whom you are close and just "chill." You may be surprised at the difference it could make.

C. Pamper yourself. Take "me" time with just you alone. Sometimes it is good just to take time to yourself. It is very important that you identify something that you can do alone based upon activities that you enjoy, or you can be adventurous and try something new. Commit to choosing something that you can do to spend time alone and create that space for "me" time. Remember, in order to be able to give your whole self to your spouse, you have to be your best self.

Make sure you focus only on yourself. Try not to allow your spouse and their absence consume you. Remember, this time is dedicated to you and pampering yourself.

How does this make you feel? Reflect on how you feel inside, knowing that you are working towards building more intimacy with your partner by focusing on yourself. Note your insights as you prepare for the next step involving you and your spouse.

Through the first action step, you should have a better idea of your strengths and weaknesses and how to improve them, by increasing intimacy through your ability to connect with your spouse. This awareness is key to the next step. Next, you will put the pieces together to see how well they fit and how you can make them fit better.

Step 2. Analyze Your Relationship

In this action step, you will use the same three tasks as above. The difference here is you and your spouse will work through this step together. As a couple, you will look at your strengths and weaknesses. See if the results surprise or confirm your thoughts about your marriage.

A. Honor each other. Take time to acknowledge the contribution that the other brings to the relationship. Let your partner know that you appreciate him or her and identify the things that you see him or her doing to keep your relationship strong. Always remember how important it is for your partner to feel appreciated, wanted and loved.

B. Enjoy the company of others close to you. Think of another couple or a group of mutual friends whom the two of you can spend time with. Socializing with other like-minded individuals can help strengthen your relationship by receiving insight from others whom you trust. This can also be an example as you are able to see how other couples interact with one another. Observing other couples can offer insight on how you could improve your interaction with your spouse. We are not saying to use the example of another couple as a guide of exactly what you should do; what we are saying is to use the example of others and apply it uniquely to your relationship in a manner that works for you and your spouse.

Scriptures: Ephesians 4:2-3 Be completely humble and gentle; be patient, bearing with one another in love. Make every effort to keep the unity of the Spirit through the bond of peace.

C. Pamper each other by spending quality time together. Focus on the amount of time you spend with each other. Sit down and analyze how much quality time is spent. Look at how much time you desire to spend together and compare it to the quality time that you can account for. Come to a mutual agreement of how much time the two of you agree to make for each other each week and hold each other to it. Also, remember your anniversary! We encourage you to make time to go away every year for your anniversary, if possible. Celebrating that time by acknowledging the fact that the two of you made it another year together is something that should be signified within your relationship and honored amongst the two of you.

How do you feel about your union, now? Keep in mind how you feel while considering the significance of making time and understanding that making love goes beyond the physical act of intimacy. Note your insights as you build your future.

Through the second action step, you should have a better idea of how to improve strengths and weaknesses within your relationship. Building on this awareness is key to the next step. Next, you will visualize where you want to go as a couple in the future.

Step 3. Create Your Future

This action step combines the previous two tasks lessons and looks forward to the future. With the insights gained from yourself and your spouse, how do you envision the next 10 years together. Understanding the importance of making time for yourself and each other may help you realize that you and your spouse have the necessary tools to develop a road map. This step contains an activity of making a plan. You will complete this activity together as a way to build your future as a couple.

Make a Plan: Where do you want to be in your marriage 10 years from now? Try not to just focus on material things, but focus on the romance and intimacy as well. Make a plan with your spouse on different things that you can do to accomplish the goals that you set together and actively work towards those goals.

Through the third action step, you should have a better idea of how work towards a brighter future. Your future should be clearer, if not continue to refine. Note your potential challenges as you begin to work towards your future.

Putting all the three steps together is easier than you think. You have worked on yourself, your relationship, and now your future. Continue to be transparent with your spouse and lead with love, while trusting God for the increase. We encourage to enjoy the journey, the good, the bad, and the ugly.

Closing Prayer

Dear God,
Please allow the passion to continue to grow as we grow more deeply in love with one another. We desire for our intimacy to be a time where we connect with each other on a physical and spiritually level.

Lord, we pray that we continue to remember that the marriage bed is undefiled (Matthew 13:4). Help us to continue to grow in love and not lose the connection, both spiritually and physically within our relationship.
In Jesus' name, Amen!

YOUR THOUGHTS FROM SESSION 5

GROUP LEADER INSIGHTS

As the group leader creates the environment, we provide additional considerations for the material contained in this workbook. We encourage you to keep the group to a size of 12 people or less. Using a comfortable place aids with open dialogue among the couples and singles gathered. There is enough information for each session to last an hour depending on your conversations, which may be stretched or shortened through time management.

One person should facilitate the group session. This will help with organization and keeping the conversation going. In addition, there may be opportunities where group members may be able to share their stories or life experiences. This is where the group leader becomes even more valuable by helping with the flow the conversation.

FURTHER THOUGHTS

ABOUT THE AUTHORS . . .

Samuel L. Hayes, Jr., Ph.D., was born in Orlando, FL and grew up abroad: Panama, Germany, Alaska, and NC; his family resides in the historic town of Fayetteville, North Carolina. He is the son of SFC (Ret.) Samuel and Marcia Hayes. Samuel adores his wife Andrea, and their three adventurous children. Sam is a soldier, a clergyman, an academic, and a businessman. He combines scholarly insights with relevant experience to develop the next generation of global strategic leaders.

Dr. Sam began his academic journey at Fayetteville State University and after enlisting in the U.S. Army, transitioned to the University of Phoenix where he graduated with a Bachelor's degree in Business Management. He continued his education, receiving a Master's in Business Administration (MBA) from American Intercontinental University, Master's in Information Strategy and Political Warfare from the Naval Postgraduate School. He earned a Doctor of Philosophy (Ph.D.) in Organization and Management with a Leadership specialization from Capella University and is pursuing a degree from Fuller Theological Seminary.

U.S. Army Lieutenant Colonel Hayes served as a Military Intelligence enlisted soldier, and as a Cavalry officer. Currently, he is serving in special operations as a Civil Affairs officer with over 22 years of combined experience. Sam is the Apostle of His Glory International Ministries, an impactful author, and the CEO of Men of Distinction Excellence and Legacy (M.O.D.E.L.) a mentorship group for young men. Sam is a member of Kappa Alpha Psi Fraternity, Inc.

To reach Sam for information on leadership, strategic design, consulting, or guest speaking please visit his **website: drsam-drdreahayes.com** or **e-mail: drsamhayesjr@gmail.com**

 **Andrea Hayes**, Ph.D., LCMHC, was raised in St. Pauls, NC, but born in Miami, FL. She is the daughter of Albert and Rosie Marsh, Sr., and sister of Albert Marsh, Jr. She is a devoted wife to Samuel L. Hayes, Jr., and the proud mother of three beautiful children, Stefone, Shirod, and Ashara. Her love for her family is indescribable.

Andrea is a former educator who is now a therapist. Her passion for helping people is the driving force behind her determination to make a difference within her local community and the Christian community, nationally and internationally.

Andrea is a proud graduate of Fayetteville State University with a bachelor's degree in English Literature. After undergraduate school, she continued her education and became a licensed middle grades educator. The passion that she has for helping students led her to eventually become a Licensed Clinical Mental Health Counselor (LCMHC) and earn her Ph.D. in Advanced Studies in Human Behavior (Counseling).

Andrea is also the Prophetess of His Glory International Ministries. She is an up and coming author, the Founder / CEO of Rivers of Peace Counseling Services, PLLC, and the founder Ladies of Vivid Elegance (L.O.V.E), a mentorship group for young ladies. She is also a member of Delta Sigma Theta Sorority, Inc.

To reach Andrea for counseling, consulting, or motivational speaking engagements, please visit her **website: drsam-drdreahayes.com** or **e-mail: drdreahayes@gmail.com.**

KEY WORD INDEX

A

Activities
    admiration for yourself, 32, 34
    assessing healthy conflict, 60
    commit to making a change, 45, 47, 49
    create a vision board, 37
    developing a road map, 22, 63
    future goals, 63
    honor yourself, 70, 71
    identify non-verbal cues, 49
    know your worth, 32, 35, 71
    make a plan, 74
    making time for yourself, 73
    pay more attention, 45, 46, 48
    record your voice, 12, 17
    review communication, 51
    smile in the mirror, 12, 14, 18
    write in a journal, 34, 36

C

Central themes
    different viewpoints, 6, 11
    faith, 22, 23, 30, 31, 47, 55
    healthy conflict, 59, 60, 62
    love and respect, 31
    love languages, 59, 60, 61
    making time, 69, 73
    miscommunication, 11
    money, 6, 11
    unhealthy conflict, 58, 60, 61, 62

S

Step
    analyze your relationship, 12, 16, 61, 72
    analyze your commitment, 34
    analyze your interaction, 48
    understand yourself, 12, 32, 35, 45, 60, 70

www.ingramcontent.com/pod-product-compliance
Lightning Source LLC
Chambersburg PA
CBHW081419080526
44589CB00016B/2603